Take Up Your Mat
AND OTHER MIRACLES OF JESUS FROM THE GOSPEL OF JOHN

BEACON HILL PRESS
OF KANSAS CITY

Take Up Your Mat

AND OTHER MIRACLES OF JESUS FROM THE GOSPEL OF JOHN

Editor
Mike L. Wonch
Director of Curriculum
Merritt J. Nielson
Writer
Montague Williams

All scripture quotations, unless otherwise indicated, are taken from the *Holy Bible, International Version*®, NIV®. Copyright © 1973, 1978, 1984, 2011 by Biblica, Inc.™
Used by permission of Zondervan. All rights reserved worldwide.

ISBN: 978-0-8341-2981-8
Printed in U.S.A.

10 9 8 7 6 5 4 3 2 1

CONTENTS

A popular way to approach the idea of miracles is to simply ask, "Do you believe in miracles?" In our cultural framework, this question can easily be the topic of a movie, a talk show, a song, or even a first date. You may have been part of a conversation based on this question, in which participants go back and forth between defending certain experiences as miraculous and explaining the experience through another means. This is often due to the way we limit our understanding of miracles simply to things that seem unexplainable in light of processes in nature or trends in history.

Theologian H. Ray Dunning points out the need for us to take a different approach and see miracles as revelatory. He says that "One does not necessarily need to restrict a miracle to an event that appears to interrupt the normal processes of nature and/or history. It may be a purely paternal happening, the timing of which impinges upon our consciousness as God's activity."[1] In fact, the question of whether or not one believes in miracles is not an overarching topic within the stories of Christian Scripture. Rather, the question is, "What do miracles mean?" Or more specifically, "How do particular miracles call us to believe in God?" Instead of trying to see how certain experiences fit in a box labeled "supernatural," we can understand miracles as those things that open our eyes to who God is.

The Bible, from Genesis through Revelation, is full of miracles. From creation to the parting of the Red Sea to the healing of the crippled man by the gate called Beautiful we see God moving and working to open our eyes to who He is. Miracles do not happen because God wants to remind us that He is in charge; rather, miracles reveal the nature of God and are designed to lead us toward Him.

The gospel of John records seven miracles performed by Jesus. These miracles had a definite impact on the lives of those who experienced them; yet, they also had an impact on the community of Christians to which John was writing. Like us, the people in John's community did not see Jesus perform these miracles first hand. Rather, they relied on the telling of the story to reveal who Jesus was. *Take Up Your Mat* focuses in on the stories of the seven specific miracles found in the gospel of John and explores their their theological meaning for us today as we seek to grow in knowledge of and faithfulness toward Christ. As you read each miracle, may your eyes be opened to the glory of God as revealed in Jesus.

Montague Williams teaches in the department of Religion and Philosophy at Eastern Nazarene College and has served as pastor to youth and families in Chicago, IL and Kansas City, MO. He is a graduate of Nazarene Theological Seminary (M.Div) and Olivet Nazarene University (M.A. and B.A.), and is completing a Ph.D. in Practical Theology at Boston University.

Turning Water Into Wine

John 2:1-11

It may seem strange that the very first miracle in John's gospel is Jesus turning water into wine. It certainly was customary in Jesus' Galilean context for wedding hosts to provide wine for guests throughout the duration of their wedding festivities, and breaking this custom would be a serious problem. However, making sure a wedding host has an abundance of wine seems to have very little significance in comparison to the other miracles of Jesus. And yet this miracle is portrayed as the "first of the signs through which he revealed his glory" (John 2:11).

Glorification

What could it mean for this miracle to reveal Jesus' glory? We often use the word "glory" in worship music and prayers to speak of God's magnificence and worthiness of praise, and the word can easily roll off our tongues without us giving it a great deal of thought. John uses his gospel narrative to help his community of Christ-followers understand certain words and concepts that are vital to Christian faith, and "glory" is one of those words. Throughout this book of the Bible, John pieces together an understanding of Jesus' glory that is grounded in Jesus' crucifixion, resurrection, ascension, and offering of the Holy Spirit to humanity. John portrays these four happenings as one complex movement that is often called Jesus' hour of glorification. For it is in this movement that Jesus fulfills God's mission of offering the world the opportunity to be made holy.

Reflect on this...

Read John 2:1-11. What are two things that stand out to you in the story of this miracle? What questions do you have?

> **Jesus fulfills God's mission of offering the world the opportunity to be made holy.**

Throughout the gospel, John slowly reveals what Jesus' hour of glorification is all about. In one scene, Jesus is at the Festival of Tabernacles in Jerusalem, and a crowd is debating with Him about His identity and authority. Some in the crowd believe He is the Messiah and some are not exactly sure. Referring to God, Jesus explains that He will eventually ascend to be with the one who sent Him. However, the listeners do not quite understand how this makes sense or how this fulfills their hope for a Messiah. So Jesus gives a deeper insight. John writes, "On the last day of the festival, Jesus stood and said in a loud voice, 'Whoever believes in me, as Scripture has said, rivers of living water will flow from within them'" (John 7:37). John explains, "By this he meant the Spirit, whom those who believed in him were later to receive. Up to that time, the Spirit had not been given, since Jesus had not yet been glorified" (John 7:38-39). With this explanation, John lets the readers know that Jesus' glory has a great deal to do with God's mission of offering the world the Holy Spirit.

In another scene, John depicts a group of people trying to figure out whether Jesus is worthy of praise. They ask Jesus to explain His own significance, but Jesus responds, "If I glorify myself, my glory means nothing. My father, whom you claim as your God, is the one who glorifies me" (John 8:54). Here, Jesus is giving a subtle hint concerning the nature of His glory. At this point in the story, the other characters do not realize that Jesus is not only fully human but also fully God. And they do not yet understand that Jesus will be crucified and resurrected. Without saying more than they could comprehend, Jesus hints at the fact that His glory is not so much about being the winner on top of the world but being one who lives out God's mission.

As the story moves forward, both the characters and we, the readers, gain a clearer understanding of Jesus' glory.

After Jesus enters Jerusalem, He is with a crowd and tells them about His upcoming death. He says, "The hour has come for the Son of Man to be glorified. Very truly I tell you, unless a kernel of wheat falls to the ground and dies, it remains only a single seed. But if it dies it produces many seeds" (John 12:23-24). He continues speaking among the crowd, "Now my soul is troubled, and what shall I say? 'Father, save me from this hour'? No, it was for this very reason I came to this hour. Father, glorify your name!" (John 12:27-28a). Here, Jesus begins to clarify that His glory is tied to His crucifixion, resurrection, and the new life offered to us through these events.

When Jesus says, "The hour has come for the Son of Man to be glorified" (John 12:23), He is saying the hour has come for His crucifixion, resurrection, ascension to the Father, and offering of the Holy Spirit to all humanity. As noted above, it is in this movement that Jesus fulfills God's mission of offering the world the opportunity to be made holy.

Reflect on this:

Read John 2:1-4. How do you think Jesus' response to Mary connects to the discussion of His "glory" and "glorification" throughout John's gospel?

Go through the gospel of John and highlight every time the word "glory," "glorification," or "hour" shows up. Consider the ways each of those stories point the reader to Jesus' crucifixion, resurrection, ascension, and offering of the Holy Spirit.

The Ultimate Purification

The question still remains as to how turning water into wine is a sign that points to Jesus' glory. When asked to bring wine to the wedding, Jesus is initially hesitant to concern himself with the task. He even suggests that it does not clearly connect with His mission to offer the world salvation. Responding to Mary, Jesus says, "Woman, why do you involve me?" . . . "My hour has not yet come" (John 2:4). But He suddenly makes a switch, and provides the wine. We would rightly be confused if John was seeking to highlight the importance of wine at a wedding. But this is not what John is emphasizing. Neither is he merely emphasizing that Jesus could perform miracles. Rather, John is emphasizing *the way* Jesus performs this miracle of getting wine to the wedding. It all comes down to Jesus' creative decision to use the six stone jars that were normally used for ceremonial washing (John 2:6).

Ceremonial washing was a common cleansing practice in Jewish tradition as a preparation for prayer and worship. For example, someone who touched an "unclean" animal or person would not be allowed into a temple nor would they be allowed close contact with someone in the community unless they first engaged in the purification practice of washing. In other words, one had to be purified prior to coming before God and close interaction with the people of God.

Water for purification would be collected from a flowing source, such as rain or a spring, and put into containers. According to the Jewish tradition, a stone jar would be the preferred container instead of a typical clay jar, because a stone jar could not become unclean and contaminate the water. Large stone jars designated for purification were rarely used for anything other than purification, and the original readers to which John was writing would recognize that it would be quite abnormal to use these jars for getting wine to a wedding. So while Jesus' use of the large stone jars may not stand out with much significance to us, it would have been an eyebrow-raiser for John's community. It would be clear to them that Jesus' use of the jars has something to do with a central message John is trying to convey through his gospel narrative.

By using the purification jars to bring wine to the wedding, Jesus is able to perform the miracle in a way that serves as a sign that reveals His glory. Throughout John's gospel narrative, Jesus is among people who are constantly questioning His identity and authority. They want to know if He is the one promised in their scriptures. They want to know if He is King of the Jews. They want to know if Jesus is the one to offer validity to the faith they have been practicing and passing on for several generations. When Jesus uses water from the purification jars, He gives the people in the gospel narrative a major clue to understanding that He is the King. And Jesus also reveals that He is even more authoritative than they expected.

They were seeking triumph for the people of God and a declaration of validity for their Jewish faith in Yahweh. Jesus offers these things, but He shows that He is also the very fulfillment of their faith and practices. He has authority beyond the practices and the various elements of those practices— such as the water for purification. In other words, He is not simply one who understands the importance of purification in Jewish tradition. Rather, He is uniquely unified with the heavenly Father, who is the very Source of purification.

Reflect on this...

How does the miracle of Jesus turning water into wine serve as a sign for Jesus to reveal His glory?

After reading this story, what thoughts do you have about the authority of Jesus?

Conclusion

Through this first miracle in John's gospel, we get a glimpse—a sign— of Jesus' unique identity and authority to fulfill Jewish tradition and offer purification to all of humanity. He will offer all of the purification needed for anyone to be a part of the people of God.

May we be reminded of Jesus' ultimate purification when we go before God in prayer and worship. And may we be reminded of His ultimate purification as we build close friendships with both Christians and non-Christians. It is Jesus' commitment to His hour of glorification that makes all of this possible.

NOTES:

2

The Healing at the Pool

John 5:1–15

Perhaps one of the most perplexing miracle stories in the gospel of John is the story of Jesus healing the man at the pool called Bethesda by telling him to pick up his mat and walk. It is common for conversations about miracle stories like this to move quickly toward a spiritual application. An example of an application might look something like this: *If there is something holding you back from journeying more faithfully with God, remember that Jesus is calling you to pick your mat and walk with freedom from the bonds of sin. So pick up your mat and walk!* There are times when this kind of application can be helpful and may be the thing that needs to be heard. However, jumping to an application can steer us away from some important things going on in the story.

Reflect on this...

Read John 5:1-15. What are two things that stand out to you in the story of this miracle? What questions do you have?

Seeing the Bigger Picture of the Story

This miracle brings together a variety of themes, but central to the story is a conversation concerning Jesus' relation to Sabbath Law. To notice this, we have to look at chapter five as a whole and pay little regard to the added subtitles used to break up the story. It is only then that we can see the narrative flow. It moves like this: Jesus heals someone on the Sabbath, Jesus is accused of breaking the Sabbath Law, and Jesus responds with a defense for His actions.

Reflect on this...

Read John 5:1-47. How do the accusations against Jesus develop into more accusations against Jesus? How does Jesus make His defense?

Unity Between the Father and the Son

To justify His work of healing the man on the Sabbath, Jesus explains that His "Father is always at work" (5:17). This gets the accusers upset for at least two reasons. First of all, Jesus speaks of God as *His* Father. It was not a new idea for Jewish people to speak of God as Father and for them to understand themselves as God's children. However, Jesus talks about His relationship with the Father as if it is different and closer than the relationship between God and the rest of God's people. Secondly, His accusers believe that Jesus is not only claiming to be uniquely close to God, but actually "making himself equal with God" (5:18). So Jesus clarifies His statements this way, "Very truly I tell you, the Son can do nothing by himself; he can do only what he sees his Father doing, because whatever the Father does the Son also does" (5:19).

What John does with this growing accusation and defense is actually an interesting play on words that is difficult to see in English. Notice that Jesus is accused of *making* himself equal with God, and then says that He is *doing* what the Father *does*. Interestingly, in the biblical Greek used here, the word for *make* and the word for *do* are the same verb—*poieo*. When John uses *poieo* to explain that the accusers thought Jesus was *making* himself equal with God, John brings one use of the verb to the front. Then, in the very next sentence, he uses the same word to speak of Jesus *doing* what the Father *does*. This may seem insignificant. We might think, *So John uses* poieo *in one sense and then uses it in another. What's the big deal?* The big deal is that John's gospel word play is a literary technique John uses throughout his gospel narrative. He intentionally uses words that have two meanings with the purpose of calling readers to consider both meanings simultaneously.[2] And John does something somewhat similar with *poieo* here. Because of the way he uses *poieo* to mean *make* in the first sentence, John's community of readers are led to consider that his use of the verb in the second sentence also means that Jesus not only does what the Father does, but also *makes* what the Father *makes*. In other words, Jesus does not have to *make* himself equal with God. In fact, what Jesus *makes* is what the Father *makes*.[3] While the religious leaders accused Jesus of grasping for a unique relationship with God, what we find is that the unity between the Father and the Son is not something at which the Son has to grasp.

John uses the controversy about healing on the Sabbath to highlight Jesus' identity as God. Jesus and the Father are not simply close; they are one. Jesus is fully God. This is a theme throughout John's gospel.

Jesus and the Father are not simply close; they are one.

In the gospel's very first sentence, John writes, "In the beginning was the Word, and the Word was with God, and the Word was God" (John 1:1). Later, he writes it another way as he portrays Jesus telling Philip, "Anyone who has seen me has seen the Father" (John 14:9). And even in chapter five, while Jesus is defending His action of healing on the Sabbath, Jesus says, "For just as the Father raises the dead and gives them life, even so the Son gives life to whom he is pleased to give it. Moreover, the Father judges no one, but has entrusted all judgment to the Son . . . Whoever does not honor the Son does not honor the Father, who sent him" (5:21-23).

Reflect on this...

Can you see the way in which John uses word play to explain that Jesus and God are indeed one?

Read John 9:1-41. In what ways does this compare with the story in John 5:1-15?

Of Sin and Suffering

The miracle story in John 5 and the miracle story in John 9 have some great similarities. But what seems like a great difference is the way each story deals with the concept of sin's relationship to suffering. In John 5, Jesus tells the healed man to "Stop sinning or something worse will happen to you" (John 5:14). This immediately lets us wonder if the man's initial suffering was due to his sinning and if Jesus is suggesting that the man would encounter a more devastating physical disability if he were to continue sinning. But the story in John 9 avoids those wonders right from the beginning. Jesus' "disciples ask him, 'Rabbi, who sinned, this man or his parents, that he was born blind?' 'Neither this man nor his parents sinned,' said Jesus, 'but this happened so that the works of God might be displayed in him'" (John 9:2-3). While the dialogue concerning sin and suffering is different in each story, they are not opposite. In fact, John 9 can be read as giving us insight into understanding John 5.

While the first story leaves us wondering if human beings suffer because of their individual sins, the second story clarifies that is not the message John is trying to send. From there, we can take a second look at what is happening in the first story. Jesus asks the man if he wants to "get well" (John 5:6) and after the man is healed, Jesus points out that he has been made well (John 5:14). Here, Jesus is speaking of the man's physical ability to walk. In that regard, he has certainly been healed. But the fact remains that this man is involved in sin. He needs a deeper healing. What's interesting is that the man did not need to stop sinning in order for Jesus to heal his physical disability. Jesus healed him despite the fact that he sins. But Jesus' goal is not simply to make this man walk. Jesus' ultimate hope is that the man's very life would be oriented toward holy living. So Jesus tells him to "Stop sinning or something worse may happen to you" (John 5:14).

> **Jesus' ultimate hope is that the man's very life would be oriented toward holy living.**

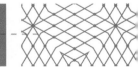

While we may be quick to think that the "something worse" means a more severe physical disability, there is really no need for this assumption. The man was unable to move for thirty-eight years. He was at the edge of a healing pool, and he could not even get himself in it. John's community of readers would see this as being one of the very worst physical disabilities. With this in mind and with the insight from John 9 in mind, it would be more appropriate to read Jesus' statement as suggesting *that something worse than a physical disability* might happen if the man continues to sin. Jesus is not threatening the healed man with a worse physical disability. Rather, by grace, Jesus is calling the healed man to a life of holy living and letting him know that the other option is to exist with no real life at all.

Reflect on this...

How might Jesus' warning to the healed man in John 5:14 be misinterpreted? What is Jesus telling this man and how is it a word of grace?

Conclusion

It can be said that Jesus intervenes amidst our moments of suffering and tells each person, *Pick up your mat and walk*. But ultimately, God is calling us to lives that are distinctly shaped by God's will and way in the world. May we receive God's conviction in our lives with humility and thankfulness.

NOTES:

3

The Feeding of the Five Thousand

John 6:5–14

One of the most recognized miracle stories in the gospel of John is that of Jesus feeding the crowd of over five thousand[4] people. One reason why this miracle story is so familiar is that it is the only one that can be found in all four Gospels. This is helpful, since one way to gain insight concerning the interpretation of a story in one of the gospels is to compare and contrast the story with how it is told in the other Gospels. Interestingly, John has some very important unique traits in his telling of this particular miracle story. The first is found in the actions and words of Jesus amidst preparing and distributing the food. In the other Gospels, Jesus uses actions and words that the original readers would recognize as actions and words typically performed and spoken during Eucharist (The Lord's Supper or Communion). In Matthew, Mark, and Luke, Jesus looks up, gives thanks, breaks the loaves, and gives them to the disciples to distribute to the crowd. In John's telling of the story, Jesus simply gives thanks and distributes the meal. The major difference is that in John's telling, he does not mention Jesus breaking the bread. So while the other gospel writers may be seeking to draw a clear connection between the miracle of feeding the crowd and the practice of Eucharist, John is seeking a different emphasis. Along with this distinction in John is the fact that Jesus distributes the food himself rather than having His disciples distribute the food. In short, this is due to John's constant attempt to tell the readers something about Jesus in particular.

Reflect on this...

Read John 6:5-14. What are two things that stand out to you in the story of this miracle? What questions do you have?

Fulfilling the Ministry of Moses

If John isn't focused on the Eucharist with this miracle story, what is he emphasizing? There are a few aspects of the story that make clear John's attempt to connect this miracle to the offering of manna in Exodus 16. The first is John's mention of the Jewish Passover early on in the story. John's community of readers would not miss out on what John is doing here. He is letting them know right away that this story will have something to do with both God's liberation of God's people out of Egypt and the stories of God's people on the Exodus journey. And as the story includes "a great crowd of people," it would be easy for the readers to imagine this crowd in a similar way to their imagination of God's people on the Exodus journey.

Reflect on this...

Read the miracle story in the other Gospels (Matthew 14:13–21; Mark 6:30–44; Luke 9:10–17). In what ways are they different? In what ways are they similar?

The second aspect that connects this miracle story to the offering of manna is found in Jesus' words after the crowd was finished eating. He tells the disciples, "Gather the pieces that are left over. Let nothing be wasted" (John 6:12). This reflects Moses' instructions to God's people concerning the gathering and eating of manna. They were to gather as much manna as they needed, but they were not allowed to leave any uneaten overnight. If they did, the food would be destroyed by maggots and wasted.

The third aspect that would support the connection of this miracle story to the offering of manna happens as John makes a connection between Jesus and Moses. After the miracle is performed and the crowd is fed, they say, "Surely this man is the Prophet who has come into this world" (John 6:14). Here, the crowd recognizes Jesus as the fulfillment of Moses' statement, "The Lord your God will raise up for you a prophet like me from among you, from your fellow Israelites. You must listen to him" (Deuteronomy 18:15). With this emphasis on manna and the overall ministry of Moses, John is once again seeking to convey a message about Jesus' authority.

Reflect on this...

Why would it be important for John to portray Jesus through the lens of manna and the ministry of Moses?

When New Testament writers seek to make clear connections to Old Testament passages, we are reminded of how important it is to view both testaments as authoritative. Think about or journal what would happen to Christian faith if Christians decided that the Old Testament was no longer authoritative.

Bread from Heaven

The connection to Moses is clear, but Jesus is not merely the new person to call upon God for manna for God's people. Jesus brings a holistic and irreplaceable salvation. Soon after this miracle story, we run into an important interaction between Jesus and the crowd He fed (John 6:25-59). John explains that the crowd was looking for Jesus, calling Him Rabbi and expressing devotion toward His teaching. But Jesus calls them out for following Him simply because He filled their stomachs. And in a somewhat humorous dialogue, the crowd continues to ask for more food while trying to cover their request in spiritual language (John 6:28-34). They specifically ask for something else like manna, so Jesus can prove once and for all that He is as authoritative as Moses.

Jesus is not simply as authoritative as Moses (John 6:32-33, 48-51). Rather, Jesus is the very sustenance of life as a whole. He is more authoritative than Moses. Jesus offers what every human being needs for a truly abundant life. Of course, the crowd in the story was left a bit confused, since Jesus talked about His own flesh as bread to be eaten. This is understandable, since the characters in the story have yet to experience Eucharist. But John's community of readers were Christians who practiced Eucharist, and they would see here that Jesus is to be understood as both the fulfillment of manna and the substance of Eucharist.

Earlier we noticed that John plays down some of the Eucharistic symbolism when distributing the food to the crowd by removing the action of breaking the bread. John was seeking to clarify that Eucharist is not simply about Jesus distributing food. Jesus is not simply the new Moses offering a new kind of bread. Rather, Eucharist is about Jesus himself being offered to all. Jesus is the bread that will be broken, so all may have life.

Jesus is the bread that will be broken, so all may have life.

Reflect on this...

Read John 6:25-52. What does Jesus teach to the hungry crowd?

Why Does Jesus Feed This Crowd?

It is important that we notice that John does not seek to spiritualize the food in this miracle story. Yes, it does call the Passover to mind, but the food does not represent anything—neither manna, nor Eucharist. Rather, Jesus is the fulfillment of manna and substance of Eucharist. What this means is that Jesus does not feed the crowd to simply make a statement. No. Jesus feeds the crowd because they were hungry. And Jesus makes it clear that He longs for hungry people to be fed.

Food is not the end-all of what Jesus offers (for He himself is the Bread of Life), but followers of Jesus are given the task of finding food for the hungry. Phillip felt a bit overwhelmed by this. He exclaimed, "It would take more than half a year's wages to buy enough bread for each one to have a bite!" (John 6:7). If he felt that way about five thousand men and their families, just imagine if he saw the number of hungry people in the world today. He would probably conclude—as many Christians today conclude—that ending hunger is simply impossible. However, this miracle story tells us that it is not impossible. In fact, ending hunger is very much the mission of Jesus.

Conclusion

The miracle of Jesus feeding the crowd of over five thousand people brings together imagery and themes that highlight Jesus' authority among God's people and His identity as the very salvation of the world. It also points us to Jesus' deep concern for those who are physically hungry for food. May we experience the grace and joy that comes with partaking in Jesus, the Bread from heaven that was broken for the forgiveness of sins. And as we consume of the Bread, may we be consumed by the Body and mission of Christ throughout the world.

Reflect on this...

There are several ways to participate in ending hunger. What is one way you can participate in this mission of Jesus?

Explore the website "Bread for the Word (www.bread.org)" and specifically think of ways in which you can participate in systemically ending hunger.

1) Jeff Pitts — sell of Tx house   TX

2) Margarets nephew John surgery shoulders today
   cousin James 2 heart valves -

3) Sheryl - valve surgery uncle Harvey
   sister Patsy " " her husband Bill cancer

4) connie - Roe's sister Parkinson

5) Sheryl - boy killed himself   mother Becca

6) pulls L in L - 7 yrs ago   Jacks→ doughter OD   son OD - suck

7) Belize team

8) Donnas mom Helen skin cancer on neck 93

9) families rash of OD

10) TMWBS

11) T hun Rany Parkinsons (Toni)

12) Becca

13) missing Ladies from BS

Jesus Walking
on the Water

John 6:16–24

The story of Jesus walking on water and meeting His disciples on a boat takes us even further in understanding Jesus' glory. In the first miracle, we saw Jesus begin the revealing of His glory by turning the water inside purification jars into wine. In the second miracle story we found Jesus revealing His identity as being one with the Father. In the third, we learned that Jesus is not simply a new prophet but the fulfillment of everything the Old Testament prophets discussed. In the current miracle story we will find that Jesus changes the way we understand our own relationship to God.

Reflect on this...

Read John 6:16–24. What are two things that stand out to you in the story of this miracle? What questions do you have? JC walked on water

as soon as JC in boat they arrived.

Why did disciples leave without JC?

mt 14:22 JC insisted they get in the boat & go

MK 6:45 JC insisted

The Disciples' Fear

The miracle of Jesus walking on water is found in Matthew, Mark, and John, but there is one important difference in the way John tells the story. In Matthew and Mark's version, the disciples do not recognize that it is Jesus on the water walking toward them in the boat. They think He is a ghost, and this frightens them. In John's telling of the story, the disciples are frightened, but they do not confuse Jesus with a ghost. In fact, they recognize Jesus. What stands out to them is not that there might be a stranger approaching them. Rather what stands out to them is that the person they have been following and getting to know is now revealed to be much more than they expected. This story takes on a whole new role in revealing God's glory.

While some video and pictorial depictions of this miracle show Jesus' feet landing parallel to an even surface of water, John's telling of the story suggests that the scene was actually not still nor calm. It was literally a dark and stormy night with choppy waves crashing back and forth. You can imagine the rough water splashing into Jesus but unable to pull Him down as He made His way closer and closer to the boat. When Jesus approaches the boat, the disciples may have already been nervous about their trip. It is easy for us to think that seeing Jesus walking on water would ease their anxiety. But imagine being nervous in the middle of a lake during storm at night, and your small group leader or Sunday School teacher shows up walking through the water toward you. While that is an amazing scene, it would be much more scary than pleasant! You would wonder what all of it means. You would wonder who she/he really is. In this case, the disciples and John's community of readers are led to consider that Jesus is God.

Reflect on this...

Read the miracle story in the other Gospels: Matthew 14:22-32 and Mark 6:45-51. What difference does it make if, in John, the disciples were frightened because they recognized Jesus as God? What were the disciples afraid of? what is going on!

Jesus' Presence

In the encounter between Moses and God at the burning bush, God told Moses that God wanted Moses to lead the enslaved Israelites out of Egypt. Moses was not sure how to explain this to the Israelites, so he asked God, "Suppose I go to the Israelites and say to them, 'The God of your fathers has sent me to you,' and they ask me, 'What is his name?' Then what shall I tell them?' (Exodus 3:13). God responded, "I Am Who I Am. This is what you are to say to the Israelites: 'I AM has sent me to you'" (Exodus 3:14). God tells Moses to refer to God as "I AM." Interestingly, when Jesus sees the fear on His disciples' faces in the boat, He speaks of himself the same way.

It is common to translate the words Jesus speaks to His disciples as "It is I; Don't be afraid," (John 6:20), but the word for "it" is not found in the original Greek version of John's gospel. Most biblical scholars of John's writings accept that what Jesus actually says to His disciples is the following: "I AM; Do not be afraid." And these scholars suggest that the phrase "I AM" (or in Greek, *Ego eimi*) plays a major role in John's theology. He uses the phrase twenty-nine times throughout his gospel narrative and portrays Jesus saying it twenty-six times.[5] In the midst of the disciples' fear, Jesus affirms to them that He is indeed God but they need not fear.

Reflect on this...

Look up and think of some of the "I AM" sayings in the gospel of John. Some, like the one in this miracle story, do not have a predicate (AM) after the phrase. They can be found in: John 4:26, 6:20, 8:24, 8:28, 8:58, 13:19, 18:5 and 7. Others do have a predicate after the phrase. They can be found in: 6:35, 6:51, 8:12, 9:5, 10:7, 9, 10:11, 14, 11:25-6, 14:6, 15:1, 5.

Different Kinds of Fear

With everything the disciples knew about how one should respond to seeing God, fear was certainly an appropriate option. God even told Moses, "You cannot see my face, for no one may see me and live" (Exodus 33:20). And yet, here was Jesus revealing himself as the I AM right before His disciples' eyes and telling them to not be afraid. Jesus' presence on the water along with His words challenged what they had previously understood about how they can relate to God.

In fact, it may even challenge what we understand about how we can relate to God. The idea of fearing God is not unfamiliar to us. In our worship gatherings, we recite passages of Scripture, such as Psalm 96:4, which says, "For great is the Lord and most worthy of praise; he is to be feared above all gods." And we make use of the language about being "God-fearing" people. The problem is that we sometimes misunderstand this idea of fear and equate it with being constantly scared of God.

The call to fear God as promoted in the psalm above and other biblical texts is a heart-felt acknowledgment that Yahweh is *the* God above all gods, and it expresses a commitment to follow Yahweh. For example, Acts 10:2 describes Cornelius as a God-fearing person. It says, "He and his family were devout and God-fearing; he gave generously to those in need and prayed to God regularly" (Acts 10:2). It does not say that he was constantly anxious that God would strike him down. Rather it is simply explaining that even though he was a Gentile, he revered Israel's God as *the* God above all gods and sought to live the life Israel's God called him to live. Unfortunately, it is common for us to neglect this call to fear God, and instead, relate to God in an anxious nervousness.

On the college campus where I teach, I have often encountered students in the midst this kind of fear, especially when they are stressed about choosing a major. Some students arrive to campus with an idea that God is supposed to make it absolutely clear to each student what their major should be. This is not a bad idea until some of the students with this understanding do not get such a clear indication concerning a major. At that point, they generate a lot of non-Christian understandings about God. They fear that God is angry with them for not being able to hear God's voice. They fear that God will stop caring about them and move on to someone else who can quickly choose a major. Or they fear that God has already abandoned them and left them to fend for themselves. But the reality is that God is saying, "I AM. Do not be afraid."

God is not calling us to be afraid of Him. Rather, God is calling us to commit to the particular way of life that is distinctly Christian, and to trust God as we encounter life experiences along the way.

God is calling us to commit to the particular way of life that is distinctly Christian, and to trust God as we encounter life experiences along the way.

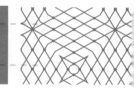

Reflect on this...

What is the difference between being a "God-fearing" person and being afraid of God? God-fearing - acknowledging God is the only God - revering God respecting - God loves us "do not be afraid" but respect & obey

love & respect

Do you have a healthy sense of fear *for God? Are there places in your life where you are wrongly "afraid" of God?*

Conclusion

When the disciples encounter Jesus on the water, what they learn is that God is very present in their lives, knows what's happening, and longs for them to make it through the bad weather safely. God is not playing chess with our lives. Rather, God hopes for us even more than we hope for ourselves. God longs for us to live lives of joy and peace, rather than anger and distress. God longs for us to relate to each other with genuine humility rather than a fend-for-yourself competitive social contract. Jesus arrives on the scene, rescues His disciples out of survival mode, and lets them know that they are loved by the Creator of the universe. May we recognize that we are deeply loved by God—the I AM. ●

NOTES:
1) Donna, Mom Helen
2) Becca
3) Tom Enfield
4) Jeff Patti
5) Jr Hi
6) Bill & Patsy week off from Chemo
7) Vicki house to sell
8)

Restoring the
Blind Beggar
John 9:1–41

If you have seen a television series like *Lost*, you would be familiar with the recent trend of prefaces before a new episode. In a deep dramatic voice, the preface would say something like, "Previously on *Lost* . . ." and then continue with quick scenes from a variety of previous episodes that are important to remember if one wants to follow the storyline of the episode about to begin. Well, if the gospel of John were such a television series, this would be an appropriate time for the voice to come in and say, "Previously in *John* . . ." and then continue with scenes from the miracle story in John 5:1-47. That's because it is important to remember that miracle story if one wants to follow the significance of the storyline in John 9:1-41.

Reflect on this...

Read John 9:1-41. What are two things that stand out to you in the story of this miracle? What questions do you have?

Read John 5:1-47. What are two things that stand out to you in the story of this miracle? In what ways are the two passages similar and dissimilar?

Toward a Verdict on Jesus' Identity

John links the stories of John 5 and John 9 by having both stories center on a controversy around Sabbath. They both begin with Jesus healing a person on a Sabbath. They both show Jesus being accused of breaking the Sabbath Law. And they both portray Jesus defending His actions through a discussion of how He is one with the Father. Some biblical scholars suggest that John links these passages with the intention of allowing the story of John 9 to offer some closure to the story of John 5.[6] More specifically, the story of John 9 allows readers to see how the religious leaders react to Jesus' identity.

Interestingly, if we keep reading the John 9 story into John 10, we find that the people accusing Jesus of breaking the Sabbath actually respond to His defense (John 10:1-21). This is different than the story in John 5, where after Jesus gives His defense, the story comes to an abrupt end. At the end of John 5, Jesus says to His accusers, "If you believed Moses, you would believe me, for he wrote about me. But if you do not believe what he wrote, how will you believe what I say?" (John 5:47). Even though Jesus asks a question, there is no response. The next sentence is the beginning of the next episode (if you will), in which Jesus feeds the crowd of over five thousand people. And readers are left in a sort of suspense, wondering how Jesus' accusers would respond to His question. Sure, the miracle of feeding over five thousand people supports what Jesus says about himself, but Jesus' question is left unanswered. After John 5, the verdict is still out on whether Jesus' accusers accept Him for who He really is.

The story that begins in John 9, however, shows the accusers trying to come to a verdict. After hearing about how Jesus performed the healing, "Some of the Pharisees said, 'This man is not from God for he does not keep the Sabbath.' But others asked, 'How can a sinner perform such miraculous signs?' So they were divided" (9:16). Then, John explains, after accusing Jesus face-to-face and listening to His defense, "The Jews who heard these words were again divided. Many of them said, 'He is demon-possessed and raving mad. Why listen to him?' But others said, 'These are not the sayings of a man possessed by a demon. Can a demon open the eyes of the blind?'" (John 10:19-21).

Notice that those who were opposed to Jesus toward the beginning of the conversation are even more adamant toward the end. First they call Him a sinner, but they conclude by declaring Him demon-possessed. And notice how those who were open to trusting Jesus toward the beginning of the conversation appear more committed to their position toward the end. At first they simply want to know how a sinner could perform the miracles. But by the end of the story, they conclude that those opposed to Jesus are flat out wrong. They say, "These are not the sayings of a man possessed by a demon" (John 10:21). Some of Jesus' accusers were becoming more and more open to trust that Jesus is truly one with the Father while others growing increasingly opposed to Jesus.

Reflect on this...

Think about the way in which John builds upon the story in John 5 with the story that begins in John 9?

Trusting in Jesus

John rejects the assumption that just because Jesus performs a miracle, people will automatically place their trust in Jesus. In fact, John is showing quite the opposite. He makes clear that trusting in Jesus requires much more than a cognitive ascent. Trusting in Jesus takes much more than proof of His identity. After reading John 5, one might think that all Jesus' accusers needed was an example of a different kind of healing on the Sabbath—one where Jesus does not have someone carry their mat. Perhaps Jesus could perform a miracle, in which all there is to consider is the wonderful gift of healing. Surely that would show Jesus' accusers how they have been missing the point. Surely that would convince them that Jesus is the fulfillment of the very Law they are accusing Him of breaking. But the miracle in John 9 does all of this, and it gives those who were opposed to Jesus all the proof they needed. And yet it only made them more adamantly resistant to Jesus and His mission.

Don't get the wrong idea here. John is not suggesting that it is predetermined that certain people will trust that Jesus is who He says He is and certain people will remain opposed. No, what John is suggesting is that when people place their sense of security in things that have nothing to do with Jesus and His mission, it becomes very difficult to give those things up and follow Him.

Later in John's gospel we find Jesus' accusers talking among themselves. They say to each other, "Here is this man performing many miraculous signs. If we let him go on like this, everyone will believe in Him, and then the Romans will come and take away both our place and our nation" (John 11:47-48). The context of Jesus was one in which the Roman political authority had a great deal of control over the practice of religion within its empire's reach. Jewish communities were allowed to practice their faith as long as it did not challenge the social and economic norms Roman authority had set in place. So certain leaders within Jewish faith were given special authoritative positions as long as they steered Jewish communities away from revolution or rebellion against Roman authority.

The problem John is highlighting is that the leaders in these special positions grew too comfortable and dependent on their closeness to power. Rather than being open to trusting in Jesus, their concern was that the Roman political authorities would say that they failed at their job. In one sense, their concern was valid. Jesus was calling His followers to live in a way that challenged the social and economic norms of the Roman Empire. The practice of welcoming the poor into authentic community and sharing resources went very much against the structures in place. And the idea of worshipping Jesus as *the* King challenged the expectation that the Roman emperor would be recognized as *the* final earthly authority. The Jewish leaders were right for thinking that the Romans would take away their positions of power and their freedom to practice Jewish faith. But what do those positions even matter in comparison to living out the life God dreams for us? These religious leaders placed so much security in their positions and false sense of freedom that they were unable to see the life Jesus was offering them.

May we learn to be blind to things that seem to matter more than trusting Jesus.

Reflect on this...

Journal about things that you depend on for a sense of security. Does your dependence on any of these things prevent you from trusting in Jesus and the life He is calling you to live?

If there is something that seems to own a great deal of your trust, consider giving it up or giving it away.

Conclusion

It is easy to grasp for security in life through work, finances, reputation, the accumulation of material, and even the bragging rights of our children's work and reputation. But the fact of the matter is that the question comes down to whether we are placing our trust in Jesus as God and committing ourselves to living the life He's calling us to live. If we cannot say yes to that, then the security we're feeling is ultimately a false one.

Jesus suggests that even though the blind man experienced the suffering of being unable to see, he was open to *seeing* Jesus for who He really is. John writes it like this: "Jesus said, 'For judgment I have come into this world, so the blind will see and those who see will become blind.'" May we learn to be blind to things that seem to matter more than trusting Jesus. And may we learn to see Jesus for who He really is—one with the Father.

1) Wendy   Linda Hassett - ~~jaw~~ jaw surgery
2) Pat Browns - Margaret daughter cancer
3) Donna - mother Helen
4) Doris - josh[12] cancer - univ of Md
5) Moses
6) Windys RBL another surgery sleeping more- pain meds.
7) Jeff
8) container   ? Run

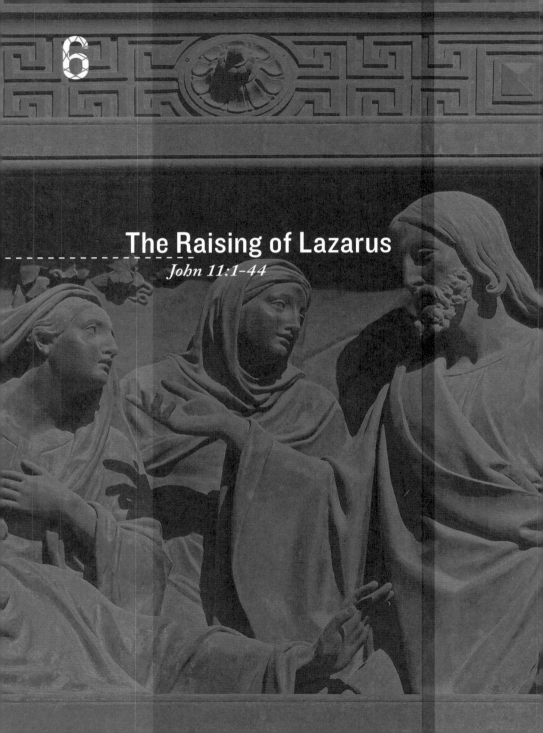

6

The Raising of Lazarus

John 11:1-44

In the gospel of John Jesus' last miracle before He is arrested and crucified is the one where He resurrects His friend Lazarus from the dead. This story is filled with theological depth and serves as the culmination of all the previous miracles. John offers readers an intimate depiction of Jesus as well as details concerning the way God in which works in our lives.

Reflect on this...

Read John 11:1–44. What are two things that stand out to you in the story of this miracle? What questions do you have?

A Few Ways of Weeping

It is in this story that we find what is known as the shortest verse in the Bible. It simply says, "Jesus wept" (John 11:35). While the verse is tiny, its implications are quite broad. There have been at least two primary ways to interpret what is happening here in Jesus' weeping. The most common understanding emphasizes Jesus' sadness concerning the death of His friend. The other emphasizes Jesus being upset about the lack of faith His closest followers have in Him. Before making any conclusions on the matter, it is important to consider reasons and implications for each of those perspectives.

Most often, we see Jesus' weeping as revealing a deep sadness concerning the death of Lazarus. Mary, Lazarus' brother, had just shown up with other Jews, and they were all weeping. There is no question that Mary and these Jews were weeping out of sadness. And what lets us conclude that Jesus does the same is the verse, which says Jesus became "deeply moved in spirit and troubled" after seeing this group of people crying (John 11:33). And it is after the group offers to show Lazarus' body to Jesus that He begins to weep. In many ways, it appears that the sight of others crying is what first allows Jesus to release the tears He had been trying to hold back. With that imagery in mind, this miracle story seems to depict Jesus struggling with very human emotions.

In fact, several biblical and theological scholars over the years have taken this passage as one that most reveals Jesus' humanity. They see Jesus displaying a deep sense of pain that often comes with the human experience of losing a friend. And if Jesus is truly sad about His friend, then one cannot deny that Jesus' existence included a distinction between the human and divine wills. In other words, if He simply knew for sure that Lazarus would be raised, then there is no reason for being sad. Sure He may have an unquestionable faith that the Father will intercede, but Jesus' sadness displays that this trust is not simply because of His divine nature. Rather, this trust depends on the same hope required of all human faith in God. Understanding Jesus' weeping as sadness for His friend clearly has important theological implications.

Others interpret this passage as Jesus' weeping because He is upset about the lack of faith His closest followers have in Him. This understanding is less common, but it does have some bearing. This view finds a different meaning of the verse, which says Jesus became "deeply moved in spirit and troubled" after seeing Mary and the Jews crying (John 11:33). The NIV translates the verb *enebrimēsato* to "deeply moved" and the verb *etaraxen* to "troubled." The NRSV translates the verb *enebrimēsato* to "greatly disturbed" and the verb *etaraxen* to "deeply moved." Both the NIV and NRSV translations are attempts to make sense of the original words while recognizing a mournful context in which Jesus' friend has died. However, a more literal translation of the Greek that does not try to adapt the words to a mournful context would say something more like "Jesus was frustrated and agitated."[7] This would suggest that rather than being moved in compassion toward a personal grieving over Lazarus' death, Jesus was intensely upset that Mary and the Jews were so sad. While this depicts a very different picture of Jesus than the first interpretation of Jesus' weeping, the dialogue in the story can support it.

When Martha greeted Jesus, her first words were, "Lord . . . if you had been here, my brother would not have died. But I know that even now God will give you whatever you ask" (11:21-22). However, as the conversation moves forward, it seems that she does not really believe that God will give Jesus whatever He asks. Jesus responded by telling her that Lazarus will rise again. One would think this would lead her to some sense of joy, excitement, or at least curiosity. But instead, she says, "I know he will rise again in the resurrection at the last day" (11:24). She didn't even think that Jesus could mean that Lazarus would be raised immediately. Jesus even goes on to explain His identity as the very resurrection and life everyone is hoping for, but she still does not get that Jesus could immediately raise Lazarus from death. Then Mary comes into the scene and greets Jesus the exact way Martha did. Mary fell at Jesus' feet and said, "Lord, if you had been here, my brother would not have died." Neither Martha nor Mary thought to say, "Jesus, now that you are here it may be possible for my brother to be waken from his death." No, instead Mary continued to weep and display sadness. This is the point where Jesus gets "frustrated and agitated" (11:33). We can imagine Jesus thinking to himself something like, "Do Martha and Mary not get it? I AM here now! What's with all of this would've and could've talk?" Jesus finds that His closest followers were able to call Him Lord and express a lack of faith in the same breath. So "Jesus wept" (11:35).

The interesting thing is the way in which the small crowd of Jewish people observing the situation gave their differing opinions on the matter. Some of them suggested that Jesus wept because of how much He loved Lazarus. And the others expressed confusion about why He could not have prevented Lazarus' death if He was able to open the blind man's eye. In those crowds, the first to give their opinions about Jesus were always the ones who refused to trust in Jesus as Lord, and the second to give their opinions were always the ones who were open to trusting in Jesus as Lord.

Fed up with the lack of faith, Jesus says, "Did I not tell you that if you believe [*trust*], you will see the glory of God? Perhaps the best way to understand Jesus' weeping is that it displays a mixture of both sadness concerning His friend's death as well as frustration concerning His followers' lack of faith. This highlights Jesus' human struggle with emotions as well as His desire to convince His closest followers about the depth of His divine oneness with the Father.

Reflect on this...

If "deeply moved in spirit and troubled" is better translated to "troubled and angry," how would that change the way you understand verses 33–35, 38–39, and 43–44?

Read John 11:1–44 with this interpretation in mind.

Changing Our Stories

Regardless of whether Jesus was sad, frustrated, or both, this miracle story also reveals the way in which God works in the lives of humans. God is constantly seeking to change the stories of suffering into stories of joy and celebration. When Jesus heard about Lazarus, He said "This sickness will not end in death. No, it is for the God's glory so that God's Son may be glorified through it" (11:4). Be careful not to take this the wrong way. Jesus is not suggesting that God goes around causing suffering just so God can heal the suffering person and get credit for it. No, Jesus is declaring that suffering, even unto death, will not be the end of the story. When we invite God into our stories of pain, God can flip the script and bring life out of it.

> When we invite God into our stories of pain,
> God can flip the script and bring life out of it.

Reflect on this...

Think about a situation in which God entered a situation and changed the ending of the story.

There are times when we long for God to change a situation, but we lack the words to pray. This can include times of suffering or even temptation. In such moments, simply pray these words, "Lord, I invite you into this situation."

Conclusion

May we have the faith to trust Jesus when He says, "I am the resurrection and the life. The one who believes in me will live, even though they die; and whoever lives by believing in me will never die" (John 11:25-26).

NOTES:

7

The Miraculous Catch of Fish

John 21:1–14

The very last miracle of Jesus in the gospel of John is a bit unique. In fact, the miracle is performed to give a message particularly to His small group of committed followers.

After Crucifixion and Resurrection

Preachers often point out that whenever a passage of scripture begins with "Then," or "Afterward," it is important to take note of the verses before the passage. This advice would be especially helpful here. In fact, it is not only important to consider the few verses before this passage. Because this passage is the fourth in a series of four stories in which Jesus appears to His followers, it is important to take note of the first three stories. Along with coming *after* those three stories, this passage portrays the miracle of Jesus that comes *after* every other miracle in the gospel of John. With that in mind, it is important to consider how this miracle is used to bring closure to the overall narrative of miracles.

After Mary Magdalene told Peter and "the other disciple" that she noticed Jesus' tomb was open, both disciples ran as fast as they could to the tomb to check out the situation. John says "the other disciple" believed the empty tomb was a sign of something good, but he further explains that both disciples "still did not understand from Scripture that Jesus had to rise from the dead" (20:9). It is amidst their confusion about His body that Jesus began appearing to these two disciples and the rest of His closest followers, showing them that He has been truly crucified and resurrected.

Jesus appeared to Mary Magdalene during her second visit to the empty tomb. The idea that He could be resurrected was so far from her mind, that she could not tell it was Him in front of her and talking with her. It was not until He said her name that she realized that He was Jesus resurrected. It didn't take any time before He commissioned her to begin spreading the news to the twelve disciples that He will be ascending to the Father (John 20:17). Jesus then appeared to the disciples one evening while they were hiding together out of fear of being persecuted and crucified just as Jesus was. All twelve disciples, except Thomas, were there in hiding. Despite their locked doors, Jesus appeared in the room and showed them His nailed hands and speared side. With this, they believed that Jesus was truly crucified and resurrected.

Through His words and actions, Jesus sought to offer *peace* amidst the disciples' fear and His presence clarified that the persecution they fear is not able to conquer them nor the Truth for which they are living (John 20:22). Jesus literally had the wounds to prove it. Of course, Thomas wanted to see these wounds for himself when the disciples told him about Jesus' appearance. In fact, he wanted more than just seeing the wounds; he wanted to touch them and know for sure they were real. Jesus appeared to him later that week and allowed him to do just that.

Realizing that Jesus was truly crucified and truly resurrected was very important for the disciples. They were literally risking their lives for Jesus, so it was important for them to see that Jesus had conquered death. Realizing that Jesus was truly crucified and resurrected was also very important for John's community of readers. They too, were being persecuted for their faith in Jesus and living out the life Jesus calls Christians to live. It is *after* the disciples in the story (and the disciples reading the story) realize that Jesus was truly crucified and resurrected that Jesus appears to His disciples by the Sea of Galilee and performs the miracle of fish.

Reflect on this:

Think about or Journal: How important is it to you (your story and way of living) that Jesus was truly crucified and truly resurrected? In other words, if you learned tomorrow morning that Jesus was not resurrected, would that make any difference in your life story or way of living?

Read John 20 and discuss Jesus' initial appearances to the disciples before the miracle of catching fish.

Drawing People into Abundant Life

We are left with an important question: Why did Jesus wait until His closest followers fully realized and accepted that He was truly crucified and resurrected? The short answer is that Jesus was making sure they would be ready to hear about the next phase of their discipleship journey, which involves carrying on His mission. Simply put, a central message in this miracle story is that Jesus calls Christians to carry on His mission in the world or, as Paul would put it, to be the body of Christ. Of course, this will take a close look at the miracle story to see how John does this.

A central message in this miracle story is that Jesus calls Christians to carry on His mission in the world

John paints a somewhat funny picture of Peter with the story. It was Peter's idea to take the boat out and go fishing. The others simply followed along for the trip. But after Jesus appeared on the beach and provided so much fish that they were unable lift the heavy load over the boat's edge, Peter immediately jumped in the water, waded his way toward Jesus, and left the group to handle the fishing on their own. There is not even a reason given as to why Peter wanted to get to Jesus so quickly. He was simply excited. The disciples on the boat ended up with a net full of large fish and Peter didn't even think to turn around to help. It was only after the group arrived to the shore and when Jesus told them to bring some fish for breakfast that Peter offered to help. That's when he climbed into the boat and took on the task of all by himself (John 21:11). Biblical scholar, Gail O'Day, even says that John portrays Peter as having a "buffoonish enthusiasm."[8]

However, John sets this up to give Peter a surprising role in the story. John writes that Peter "climbed back into the boat and *dragged* the net ashore" (John 21:11). The NRSV says that Peter "*hauled* the net ashore." The actual verb here is *helkō*. Interestingly, the other times that John uses *helkō* is when he portrays Jesus welcoming people to a life of faith. In those cases, the verb is translated to *draw*. In John 6:44, Jesus says, "No one can come to me unless the Father who sent me *draws* them . . ." In John 12:32, Jesus says, "And I, when I am lifted up from the earth, will *draw* all people to myself." It would certainly be strange to translate Jesus' words to say, "No one can come to me unless the Father *drags* them," or that Jesus will *drag* all people to himself. But it would also be inappropriate to overlook John's use of the verb in the miracle story as if there was no connection to Jesus' earlier statements. Considering the way John uses wordplay to make theological statements, it is appropriate to conclude that this miracle has symbolic significance, suggesting that Peter and the rest of the disciples will participate in God's mission to *draw* people toward faith in Christ.[9]

This understanding connects well with the next scene, in which Jesus tells Peter, "Take care of my sheep" (John 21:16). And it builds upon the earlier scene when Jesus appears to the disciples as they were hiding from their persecutors. Jesus ". . . breathed on them and said, 'Receive the Holy Spirit. If you forgive anyone's sins, their sins are forgiven; if you do not forgive them, they are not forgiven'" (John 20:22-23). In that moment, Jesus made it possible for His disciples to participate in His mission. And in the moment of Peter *drawing* in the heavy load of fish Jesus provided, it is made clear to John's community of readers that the disciples will participate in the task of welcoming people to a life of growing Christlikeness.

This does not mean the task falls completely on the shoulders of Jesus' disciples. In fact, there wouldn't have been any fish without Jesus providing it, and Peter would not have thought to *draw* the fish if Jesus did not call for it (John 21:5-6). It does suggest, however, that Christ's disciples are empowered and called to join God in the work of welcoming all people to the life God hopes for us.

Conclusion

"Jesus performed many other signs in the presence of his disciples, which are not recorded in this book. But these are written that you may believe that Jesus is the Messiah, the Son of God, and that by believing you may have life in his name" (John 20:30-31). ●

Reflect on this:

How does John's use of helkō in this miracle story symbolically point Christians to participating in God's mission in the world?

How do (could) you or your group participate in drawing people toward a life of Christlikeness? How are you being called to participate in God's mission in the world?

NOTES:

Notes

1 H. Ray Dunning. *Grace, Faith, and Holiness.* (Kansas City: Beacon Hill Press of Kansas City, 1988), 261.

2 Gail R. O'Day. "The Gospel of John," in *NIB Commentary.* Vol 9. (Nashville, TN: Abingdon Press, 1995), 687.

3 Craig Keener, *The Gospel of John: A Commentary.* Volume 1. (Peabody, MA: Hendrickson Publishers, 2003), 648.

4 This number represents the men; women and children were not included in the figure.

5 Gerald Sloyan. *John.* (Atlanta, GA: John Knox Press, 1988), p. 100-01.

6 Martin Asiedu-Peprah. *Johannine Sabbath Conflicts as Juridical Controversy.* (Tubingen: Mohr Siebeck, 2001).

7 I suggest this translations after considering discussions in, Keener, 846; and O'Day, 690.

[2] Augustine's Sermon on Revelation 5:5, quoted in, Alister McGrath. *Theology: The Basics.* Third Edition. (Oxford: Blackwell Publishing, 2012), 96.

8 Gail O'Day, 858.

9 Craig Koester, *Symbolism in the Fourth Gospel: Meaning, Mystery, Community.* Second Edition. (Minneapolis, MN: Fortress Press. 2003), 135.

Further Reading

Rick Williamson. *NBBC, 1, 2, & 3 John: A Commentary in the Wesleyan Tradition.* (Beacon Hill Press of Kansas City)

Gary M. Burge. *Interpreting the Gospel of John: Guides to New Testament Exegesis.* (Baker Books)

Craig Koester. *Symbolism in the Fourth Gospel: Meaning, Mystery, Community.* Second Edition. (Fortress Press)

Other Dialog studies also available!

ELEPHANTS IN THE CHURCH
Conversations We Can't Afford to Ignore

Elephants in the Church centers the conversation around the difficult topics of politics, prejudice, addictions, abuse, sexual sin, materialism, and how to create a safe and open atmosphere for conversations within the Church.

PARTICIPANT'S GUIDE ISBN: 978-0-834I- 2979-5
FACILITATOR'S GUIDE ISBN: 978-0-834I-2985-6

CHRISTIAN DISCIPLINES
Creating Time and Space for God

Disciplines that contribute to the transformation of our hearts and lives enable us to increase our capacity to love God and others. See how *reading, praying, connecting, fasting, giving,* and *receiving* are important practices to integrate into your daily walk with God.

PARTICIPANT'S GUIDE ISBN: 978-0-834I- 2980-I
FACILITATOR'S GUIDE ISBN: 978-0-834I-2986-3

Available online at DialogSeries.com

Animal Helpers

Bob McCall

Rigby®

A Harcourt Achieve Imprint

www.Rigby.com

1-800-531-5015

People often work together.
They help each other
- get food,
- stay safe, and
- keep clean.

Many animals also work together.

The crocodile opens its mouth
for the plover bird.
The bird gets dinner.
The crocodile gets clean teeth.

plover bird

The oxpecker bird lives on big animals, such as zebras, rhinos, or deer.
The oxpecker eats **insects** that get on an animal's skin and in its ears.

The bird also **alerts** the big animal if danger is near.

oxpecker bird

Pilot fish follow a shark all around.
The shark **protects** the pilot fish
from bigger fish.
The pilot fish eat the shark's
leftover food.

Some pilot fish eat crabs and worms
that are on the shark.
Pilot fish help keep the shark **healthy**.

pilot fish

Cleaner shrimp stay in one spot
and wait for fish to come by
to be cleaned.
The shrimp eat dirt and old skin
off the fish.
This helps keep the fish clean.

Moray eels even let the shrimp
clean their teeth.

cleaner shrimp

The clown fish and sea **anemone**
help each other.
Big fish follow the clown fish
to the anemone.
The anemone stings the big fish.
Then the clown fish and anemone
eat the big fish.

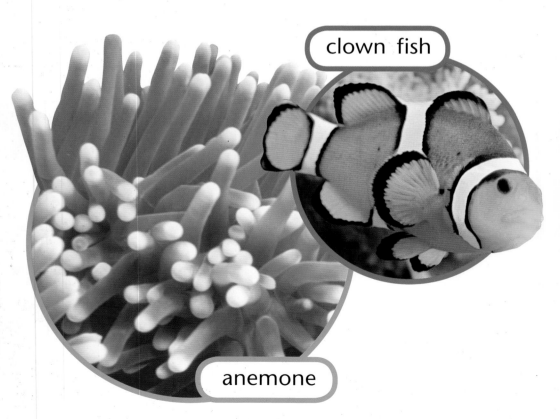

clown fish

anemone

Aphids are tiny insects that eat plants and flowers.
Aphids make a sweet **liquid.**
This liquid is called honeydew.
Ants love honeydew, so they look for plants with aphids.

Ants take a group of aphids to the ant nest at night to protect them.
During the day, the ants **herd** the aphids from plant to plant.

ant

aphid

Ants help some caterpillars become beautiful butterflies. Red ants take these caterpillars to the ant nest. The ants feed the caterpillars. The caterpillars live in the ant nest for a long time. Then the caterpillars are ready to become butterflies.

The butterflies have to get out of the ant nest fast. The ants feed caterpillars, but they eat butterflies! Even best friends don't always get along!

butterfly

ant

caterpillar

15

Glossary

alerts tells that danger is near

anemone a sea animal that looks like a plant but eats fish for food

healthy feeling well and not sick

herd to make a group of animals move from one place to another

insects small animals with six legs and three body sections

liquid something that can flow, like water

protects tries to keep something or someone safe